Herculaneum: the excavations,
local history and surroundings

Ministero per i Beni e le Attività Culturali
Soprintendenza Archeologica di Pompei

Herculaneum: the excavations, local history and surroundings

Maria Emma Antonietta Pirozzi

Electa Napoli

Electa Napoli

Editing
Silvia Cassani
Paola Rivazio

Graphic design
Paolo Altieri

Art director
Enrica D'Aguanno

Graphics
Flavia Amendola

English translation
Mark Weir

Photographic references
Archivio Fotografico
della Soprintendenza
Archeologica di Pompei;
Alfredo and Pio Foglia: cover;
pp. 30, 41, 48, 51-55, 57-63,
65-66, 68-69, 71-75
Luciano Romano: pp. 86-87
Capware: pp. 34-35
© for pictures
by Soprintendenza Archeologica
di Pompei

*The collaboration of the following
is gratefully acknowledged*
Cecilia Misiani and Maurizio
De Fulgentiis, Dipartimento
del Turismo - Presidenza
del Consiglio dei Ministri;
Adriano de Rose
Giuseppe Mastrolorenzo
Elisabetta Pace

This publication has benefited
from a contribution from
the Structural Funds
of the European Community,
Programma Operativo
Multiregionale Turismo
sottoprogramma I, misura 5,
della Presidenza del Consiglio
dei Ministri - Dipartimento
Turismo

How to get to Herculaneum
Modern Ercolano can be
reached by car on Autostrada
A3 Napoli-Salerno; by train
with the Circumvesuviana
from Corso Garibaldi or Piazza
Garibaldi, Napoli-Sorrento
or Napoli-Poggiomarino; also
by train with Ferrovie dello
Stato to Portici-Granatello;
or by trolley bus from
Naples, Piazza Garibaldi

How to get to Vesuvius
Autostrada A3 Napoli-Salerno,
exit Ercolano or Torre
del Greco. To reach the
Observatory, take the minor
road from either Pugliano or
Montedoro. Continue on foot
to the crater. Alternatively you
can climb up Monte Somma
and Punta Nasone from
Sant'Anastasia or Somma
Vesuviana following the route
marked by the WWF for Santa
Maria a Castello

First edition 2000
Printed in Italy
© 2003 by **Ministero per i Beni
e le Attività Culturali**
Soprintendenza Archeologica
di Pompei
electa napoli srl
Gruppo Mondadori Electa s.p.a.

Contents

Preface

The chief responsibility of the Superintendence is the conservation of the archaeological monuments placed under its care. This requires a thorough knowledge of these monuments, from both the scientific and technical points of view. For our non-specialist visitors, the results of our work lie in what they see in front of them; everyone can compare what they see with their notions and expectations, and in so doing verify or increase their knowledge of the ancient world.

Scientific research is by its very nature the domain of a few specialists. Yet the communication of the findings of this research offers limitless possibilities, whose scope and variety are now clearer than ever before. It is not just a question of practical applications, which in the case of archaeology means the approach to restoration. This communication must be used to broaden popular culture, increase people's awareness of our heritage of historical and cultural artefacts, and ultimately extend each individual's patrimony of notions and information. It is no easy matter to plan and put into practice this kind of communication: the first requisite is to identify the potential "users". Society today is characterised by a complex stratification of knowledge and interests, and this means that we have to cater for many kinds of user, establishing the topics which will be of interest to each kind. We then go on to choose the type of language, illustrative apparatus, background, visual impact and so on which are appropriate.

Drawing up and pursuing such a project requires specialised knowledge, specific professional experience, a great deal of patience, deep humility and unswerving commitment, not to mention the intelligence involved in sensing the needs of the society one is trying to cater for. The brief series of publications we are offering to the public hardly matches up to this ambitious, and at the same time inescapable, blueprint. We have tried to identify the topics, objectives and approaches on the basis of our experience, which is undoubtedly a reliable touchstone, although it does not always correspond to what scientific criteria would dictate. In pursuing this goal we have been comforted by the thought that what we are producing is merely a prototype, not a definitive finished product. Our hope is that the reactions of our readers will provide us with extensive and reliable feedback, enabling us to improve these instruments of communication.

Pietro Giovanni Guzzo
Archaeological Superintendent of Pompeii

Foreword

As part of an editorial initiative aimed at extending people's knowledge of the archaeological site of Herculaneum and the surrounding territory, this essential guide to the coastal area at the foot of Vesuvius, with Herculaneum at its heart, provides visitors with a broad knowledge of the territory, and should make their visit more stimulating and meaningful.
The archaeological site of Herculaneum constitutes an urban archaeological park adjacent to the built-up area of the "Golden Mile". It is indissolubly bound up with the discovery of the site and the revelation this afforded of life in ancient times. In this volume we hope to give a broad spectrum of visitors an awareness of the context as a whole. It is high time that the archaeological site, the royal palace in Portici, the Vesuvian villas, the Vesuvius National Park and, last but by no means least, the historical centres of Resina and Torre del Greco ceased to be regarded as so many attractions in a touristic venue that leaves much to be desired and came to be seen as the product of a variety of cultural expressions that inspired their creation and existence. Today at last they can benefit from the determination to communicate and inform, in the light of a modern approach to safeguarding and exploiting our cultural heritage, which will lead to a more informed and qualified use.

Valerio Papaccio
Project manager

Satellite picture of the Campanian plain

Geographical features

The name *Campania* is first found in a work by the Greek author Pseudo Scilace, dating from the second half of the 4th century B.C., and in the Roman writer Varro. It describes a crescent-shaped volcanic plain at the foot of the Appennine escarpment, extending from the River Volturno to the Monti Sorrentini. Its coastline, originating in a tectonic hollow, faces the Tyrrhenian Sea and extends from Mondragone down to Castellammare di Stabia. The southern end of this plain is a distinct geographical entity with its own surface characteristics and natural features. Southwards, towards the Bay of Salerno, it culminates in the mountain ridge featuring the peaks of Albino, Amarrato and Sant'Angelo. The headland of the Sorrento Peninsula reaches out into the sea, terminating in Punta della Campanella, with the island of Capri lying just off it. Eastwards the River Sarno divides the Valley of the Sarno from the Sannio; westwards, the plain opens out onto the Bay of Naples. Northwards, there is a breach in the surrounding escarpment between Vesuvius and the Monti di Palma through which the Valley of the Sarno is linked to the northern end of the Piana Campana. The Sarno flows through the whole length of this valley from east to west.

The territory has traditionally been described as a *locus amoenus* for the benevolence of its climate, the fertility of the soil and its magnificent panorama. It is largely made up of volcanic rock formations coloured grey or rust-brown (which are morphologically different from the yellow-ochre tufa rock of the Phlegrean Fields). This is the product of many centuries of volcanic activity in both explosive and effusive forms, giving the area an unmistakable geomorphological identity.

In the course of time the volcanic formations, the result of both lava and pyroclastic deposits, have been covered by luxuriant woodlands all the way from the upper slopes of Monte Somma-Vesuvius down to the coast with its fertile farmland. In particular the wine grown in the vineyards has long been a staple element in local commerce, being sold both locally and for export. The undergrowth has a rich flora featuring large bushes of broom and prickly pear and extensive pinewoods, and extends over the solidified lava from recent eruptions.

The tectonics of the area has been determined by the successive eruptive cycles of Vesuvius. In ancient times the major settlements were Herculaneum, which was primarily residential; Pompeii, a riverside port on the River Sarno; Stabiae, favoured for its hot springs and overlooked by the plateau of Varano; and Oplontis, now Torre Annunziata, a favourite location for patrician and rustic villas, which were built all round the eastern shore of the Bay. This is the background to the ever-increasing anthropisation which has taken place over the centuries from halfway up Vesuvius (as high as 600 m. a.s.l.) down to the seashore.

Dense urbanisation of the coast has been a typical feature through all the ages, the present day included. The various types of villa built in ancient times – rustic, maritime and for leisure or "*otium*" – together with the urban residences and bathing establishments, all illustrate the intensive development that took place above all during the first decades of Imperial Rome, and then again in the 18th century, culminating in the high levels of urban density which now cause serious congestion.

The Volcano

The ample bulk of Vesuvius, which has featured in every iconographic representation of Naples over the centuries and

also in the travel diaries of numerous visitors including Goethe, Chateaubriand and Stendhal, actually comprises two mountains: Vesuvius itself, which has varied in height as a result of successive eruptions, but which today measures 1277 metres, and Monte Somma, 1110 metres high. The latter surrounds Vesuvius, which actually rests on it, so that we have an example of an "enclosure volcano". At one stage the Great Cone of Vesuvius thrust up through the ancient crater of Monte Somma, although the two mountains are not concentric: Vesuvius is off-centre with respect to its girdle. The two have gradually

blended into each other over the centuries so that the shapely
bulk familiar to us today is very different from how it looked
in Pliny's time. This process, made up of a sequence of
eruptions and periods of dormancy with alternating demolition
and rebuilding, can be summarised in three phases:
– formation of the volcanic basis of Monte Somma through the
accumulation of layers of lava and pyroclastic deposits;
– the collapse of the southern end of Monte Somma, which
came about approximately 1700 years ago as a result of volcanic
and tectonic phenomena, creating the Atrio del Cavallo and the
Valle dell'Inferno;
– formation of the Great Cone.
Following each eruption Vesuvius was decapitated but acquired
a more stable base, making it possible to support an
increasingly high Great Cone. The origins of Monte Somma go
back some 25,000 years. In general, prolonged periods of
dormancy have been followed by explosive or "Plinian" eruptions.
The Great Cone is the result of centuries of modest eruptions
of both the explosive and effusive types in which lava seeps out.
There is a divergence of opinion about what the volcano looked
like before the eruption in 79 A.D.: there is some historical
evidence that it had two crowns, but it may have had only one.
The first "historical" eruption is reckoned to be the one in 79
A.D., although it is thought that Vesuvius was active at the time
of the Greeks' first landing on the coasts of Campania.
Diodorus, referring to Timeus before him, states that the
Campanian plain was called *Phlegrea* "from the mountain
known today as Vesuvius, which once spewed out a great river
of fire, as Etna does in Sicily; still today there are many signs
of this ancient conflagration". The Italic name "Vesuvius" is
similar in meaning to the Greek name for the volcano, which
according to Timeus meant "mountain of flames".

In that period Vesuvius cannot have had the profile we know today. As many writers concur, there was the single crest of Monte Somma, which became double following the eruption of 79 A.D. In 19 A.D. Strabo wrote in his *Geografia*: "It is a mountain covered with fertile soil, which seems to have had its top cut off horizontally, forming an almost level plain which is completely sterile and ash coloured, on which you come across caverns full of cracks made of blackened rock, as if it had been subjected to fire. Thus one can surmise that there used to be a volcano there, which died out once it had consumed all the inflammable material that fed it".

Apart from Pliny the Younger, who gave us our only eye-witness account of the eruption in 79 A.D., the Greek and Latin authors who wrote about Vesuvius were more interested in its mythological interpretation than a scientific description. Virgil, Martial and Suetonius bestowed lustre and mystery on the topos by identifying it with Vulcan's smithy or locating the realm of the Giants in its gloomy caverns and the abduction of Proserpine on its slopes. Leaving this literary tradition aside, the first historical records of the mountain we possess which are reasonably reliable and detailed (although Strabo's account remains the first accurate description) are the narratives concerning Spartacus and his battle for the liberty of his fellow slaves fought in part on the slopes of Vesuvius in 73 B.C. The *fauces cavi montis* referred to by Florus, down which the Thracian rebel lowered himself to make his escape, correspond to the Atrio del Cavallo, the region in which Vesuvius was formed. These descriptions are corroborated by the wall painting discovered in 1779 in Herculaneum (according to A. Nazzaro's recent hypothesis, which some dispute) and another that came to light in Pompeii in 1879 showing Vesuvius and Bacchus. Other scholars, however, such as Beloh (in 1879) and

Nissen (1883), maintain that the mountain already had a double crown before the eruption in 79 A.D.

In any case, by 79 A.D. the inhabitants of Pompeii, Herculaneum and Stabiae believed Vesuvius to be extinct, and were totally unprepared for the eruption that took place on August 24th of that year. This was all the more violent for the long period of dormancy that had preceded it, and it completely transformed the region. Since that event there have been many other eruptions, but only the one that took place in 1631 came anywhere near it in magnitude. This latter began on December 16th, and once again caught the local residents totally unawares, coming after more than 500 years of dormancy. The cone had grown much taller, surpassing the top of Monte Somma, while its slopes were so densely wooded and its pastures so lush that it featured as a bucolic topos in the writings of the humanists Pontano and Sannazaro. The year 1631 marked the beginning of a systematic study of the volcano's activity and in particular its eruptions. Much more recently, 1995 saw the creation of the Vesuvius National Park, with a protected area of 8490 hectares.

Chronology of the main eruptive phases and types

– 62 A.D.: earthquake that affected Herculaneum, Pompeii, Stabiae and Naples;
– 79 A.D.: eruption, destroyed Pompeii, Herculaneum and Stabiae;
– eruptions in 203 (recorded by Dione Cassius who witnessed it from Capua), 472 and 512 (described by Cassiodorus and Procopius, who for the first time records lava flows);
– December 16th 1631, 3,000 people engulfed by lava. Naples was spared: the spire in Piazza Sforza was erected in thanksgiving to San Gennaro. From this time onwards, thanks

in particular to the vigilance of local Jesuits, Vesuvius was kept
under constant observation;
– 1694: eruption with lava flowing out of the crater;
– 1767: lava arrived as far as San Giorgio a Cremano, stopping
at the outskirts of Naples;
– 1794: Torre del Greco destroyed;
– 1906: eruption which increased the diameter of the crater by
300 metres;
– 1933: seismic tremors heralded a new eruption, with lava
appearing on June 3rd;
– 1944: a violent explosion announced Vesuvius's last active
phase to date; following the eruption the familiar plume of
smoke disappeared.
Investigation of the quantity of lava erupted has enabled
scientists to identify three main categories of eruption:
a) catastrophic or Plinian eruptions such as the one in 79 A.D.,
with thousands of tons of lava pouring out, characterised by the
emission of large quantities of pumice and ashes accompanied
by thick layers of pyroclastic material and mud flows;
b) explosive or sub-Plinian eruptions which took place in 472
and 1631, characterised above all by blocks of debris, ash and
lapillus, particularly pumice, raining down;
c) modest eruptions like the one in 1906 in which activity is
predominantly effusive or a combination of effusive and
eruptive and lava flows or spouts occur.

The Vesuvian Observatory

The Vesuvian Observatory was set up in the years 1841-1845 at
the express wish of the king Ferdinando II and inaugurated on
September 28th 1845 during the VII Congress of Italian
Scientists. The neoclassic villa contains an interesting mineral
collection and a well stocked library. Nowadays it is a centre

for research in which scientific instruments and rock and
mineral samples are on permanent exhibition, while its operative
functions have been transferred to Naples.

The funicular

This was designed in 1870 and inaugurated in 1880. Its track
was 800 metres long, rising from 800 metres to 1180 metres
a.s.l. It ceased to function in 1944, when the station was the
first casualty of the lava flow. In 1951 the Società Autolinee
Vesuviane began work on a chairlift which was completed in
1953 and was in operation until 1984. At the moment there is a
project, lurking in the recesses of the Campania Regional

Authority, for a much more practical method of conveying visitors up the mountain by means of an overground funicular like the ones in use in Naples.

Local wine

In ancient times Vesuvius was viewed as one large vineyard: a famous wall painting found in Pompeii shows that it was sacred to Bacchus, who made his home on its slopes, together with his retinue of nymphs and satyrs. It was associated with merry-making and inebriation, and Pliny, among others, was fulsome in his praise of the wines from Vesuvius. The location is ideal for viticulture on account of its soil, rich in phosphorous and alkalis, and climate. The wines produced are the celebrated "Lacryma Christi", lauded by Stendhal and Charles de Brosses; "Greco di Torre", a favourite of Montesquieu; "Greco di Tufo", recipient of many prizes, which takes its name from the vine imported from Pelasgia in Thessalia; and "Greco di Somma", mentioned by Petrarca, who states that the name "Greco" indicated its origin in Magna Graecia.

Climate and vegetation

The geographical situation of the territory stretching from the coast up to the cone of Vesuvius is favoured with a climate that is excellent for both habitation and certain types of cultivation. The annual average temperature ranges from 16.4°C down at sea level to 13.3°C up at the Observatory. The hottest months are July and August, the coldest January, and there is limited daily variation between minimum and maximum temperatures. Annual rainfall is about 845 mm on the coast and 960 mm on the mountainside. The year can be divided into two periods, the rainy season running from October to April and the dry, sunny season from May to September. Particularly down at sea level farming can be actively pursued throughout the year, producing such profitable crops as vegetables and carnations, the later cultivated in glasshouses.

The area is rich in various quite distinct species of vegetation. In the mountain sector holm oak, strawberry tree, laurel, rosemary, pine and xerophile ginesta are found; the intermediate sector is primarily characterised by timber and seedcrops, while the coastal zone is entirely given over to herbaceous species. In the first of these sectors, where the lava has disintegrated, both the domestic and maritime pine have taken hold and formed extensive pine forests. Further down, where the lava is interspersed with banks of ash and lapillus which have been farned, you find the typical lush Mediterranean species such as bay-laurel.

Ercolano

Moden Ercolano is a small seaside town in Campania, situated half-way along the coast road that runs from Naples to Pompeii and on to the towns of Nocera, Castellammare and Sorrento. Its origins go a long way back to times when history and myth are hard to distinguish, suggesting varying hypotheses. The Greek toponym can be associated with the first Greek adventurers to set foot in Campania, coming from the island of Rhodes. In its form as pronounced by the Oscans this was *Hereclena*, hence *Hereklanon* and in popular usage *Herculanum*.

Chiarini believes that the toponym derives from the Phoenician, "since in that language *Heracli* means *ardens ignis*, indicating the volcanic nature of the soil where Ercolano was founded".

Dioniges of Halicarnassus ascribes the town's foundation to the mythical hero Hercules, who he represents making a sacrifice to the gods here on his journey back from Iberia. Apart from the mythical aspect, this account indicates that the town was originally Greek. It was common for the Greeks to pay homage to Hercules, and there have been numerous finds on the site of Herculaneum which show that this cult did exist here. Amedeo Maiuri maintained that it was the Greek inhabitants of nearby Neapolis who developed this location in order to strengthen the settlements in the hinterland by implanting some outposts along the coast. The urban layout is undoubtedly Greek, and is actually more conventional than that of Pompeii. The streets are straight and form a grid pattern: the *decumani* run parallel to the coast, from north-east to south-west, and are intersected at right-angles by the *cardines*, so that the town is divided up into regular blocks or *insulae*.

The historian Sisenna, writing in the first half of the 1st century B.C., describes Herculaneum as "a fortified town with modest walls, on a promontory overlooking the sea with two streams on either side of it". This can be verified in the map drawn by Francesco La Vega, which gives an idea of its topography. It was built on steeply sloping ground, ending in a cliff face where the headland fell away sharply. The houses were built on terraces which descended to the edge of the cliff, affording a fine view out over the bay. The built-up part was linked to the port by means of vaulted passages, leading from the *cardines* down to the waterfront.

Frenkel gives the following description: "Occupying the most picturesque location in the whole of the Parthenopean bay, with the clear, calm, fragrant sea to the south and the luxuriant slopes of Vesuvius, always green and decked with flowers, to the north, *Herculea urbs* stood transfigured in sunlight, in forest green and marine blue, making a superb sight with its splendid flanks (the suburbs of Torre del Greco to the east and Portici to the west) dotted with villas and woods, truly surpassing all imagination, at the heart of the other six incomparable marvels of this region: Pompeii, Stabiae, Capri, Ischia, Naples and the Phlegrean Fields". Strabo was enchanted by the view from the castle which stood square to the south-westerly wind. He commented that nowhere could a period of residence and "*otium*" (leisure) be more agreeable, and in fact many historians have referred to it as the "ideal resort" for the Roman gentry. However, on August 24th 79 A.D. a thunderclap shattered the peace of a drowsy summer's day, and the cloud of smoke and flames which erupted from the volcano completely blocked out the sun, causing an eerie darkness. It must have been a truly terrifying sight. In the words of Dione Cassio: "People believed that the giants had returned and the world was plunged once again into chaos, to be consumed by fire".

Both Pompeii and Herculaneum were buried by the eruption, as Pliny the Younger described at length in letters to Tacitus. Pompeii is approximately 15 km from Vesuvius, and was buried to a depth of six metres beneath the lapillus, pumice and ash expelled by the volcano and borne by the wind. Herculaneum, on the other hand, is only 7 km from the volcano: it was engulfed by a pyroclastic flow moving fast and at very high temperatures, and by the time it solidified the town was buried to a depth of twenty metres. The mixture of ashes and water underwent a process of lithification which turned them into compact tufa rock, and this ensured the conservation of the walls of houses above the first storey and also wood and other organic substances. The blast, accompanied by scorching gases, was fatal to anyone and anything in its path: all the inhabitants were asphyxiated and then hermetically sealed, together with their possessions and all other artefacts, in the pyroclastic layer. We have evidence of marble statues being ripped from their plinths, to be found in pieces at considerable distances from where they had stood. One example is the statue of the proconsul M. Nonius Balbus, which we know to have stood in the square in front of the Suburban Baths.

Visitors to Herculaneum can see not only the remains of part of the ancient town but also the largest collection in existence of organic materials from the Roman world, including skeletons, materials and furnishings. The latter are truly unique, and give a direct insight into the day-to-day life of our ancestors.

Brief history

Strabo, the geographer who lived in the Augustan age, maintained that the first inhabitants of Herculaneum were the Oscans, who called the whole region *Opicia* (land of work), and that this settlement, comprising only a few houses, soon came under the influence of the Greeks who had founded a colony in the nearby Neapolis. In the 6th century B.C. the arrival of the Etruscans led to a significant increase in the trade passing through this sea port. In 474 B.C. the Etruscans were defeated by the Greeks, who became masters of the whole arc of the Bay from Cuma round to Punta Campanella; the domination of first the Etruscans and then the Greeks played an important part in the development of Herculaneum. During the 5th century B.C. the Greeks were supplanted by the Samnites, who adopted many features of the Hellenistic way of life and made their own contribution to developing the town and making it look attractive, with some touches of genuine refinement. The Oscan-style house, rather squat and self-contained with doors and windows kept to a minimum, was enlarged and embellished; the plot of land next to it became first a garden and then a *quadriporticus* (a four-sided colonnade or covered walkway) adorned with a colourful decorative scheme. An upstairs floor might be added, providing servants' quarters and storage space, and subsequently a second floor above this. Following the Samnite conquest, Herculaneum was part of the Nucerine League, and when in 307 B.C. it, together with *Nuceria*, came under Roman rule, it remained faithful to Rome until the outbreak of the Social War. When Papius Mutilus invaded the Sarno Valley, Herculaneum, like *Stabiae* and *Surrentum*, rebelled against Roman domination. In 89 B.C. Titius Didius, Sulla's legate, reconquered the town, which became a Roman *municipium*. Like the other towns which had been part of the Nucerine League, Herculaneum was enrolled in the *Menenia* tribe, and its time as a *municipium* was the most prosperous period in its history. It was provided with streets, sewers, palaestras, basilicas and a splendid theatre. In the earthquake of 62 A.D. the town was badly damaged; rebuilding had begun, with the support of government subsidies, when the eruption of 79 A.D. completely effaced it, and subsequently this region was included in the territory of *Neapolis*. Although Pompeii is better known, being larger, more populous and more important commercially, it is actually Herculaneum which stands at the centre of this happy conjunction of human and natural achievements embodying a harmonious equilibrium with the environment amidst an extraordinarily beautiful landscape. It was certainly no coincidence that it should be the chosen residence for such aristocratic Roman families as the *gens* Nonia of *Nuceria*, the consul Appius Claudius Pulcher from Rome and also L. Calpurnius Piso, the consul to Macedonia who had a passion for Epicurean philosophy. Yet it was not just the presence of important personages which ensured the standing of Herculaneum: a safe harbour, rich fishing, vines in abundance giving wine praised by Martial, and the intensive farming of wheat and oil introduced by the Romans which led to the network of smallholdings known as *villae rusticae*, all played their part.

History of the excavations

The discovery of Herculaneum came about by chance. In 1709 Prince D'Elbœuf, who had come to Naples with the Austrian army which defeated the Spanish, purchased a villa overlooking the sea to the west of the Granatello harbour from a religious order. During the digging of an artesian well some marble fragments from the proscenium arch of the theatre of Herculaneum were turned up, duly presented to the Prince in 1710-1711, thus inaugurating not only the discovery of Herculaneum but also its spoliation. Excavations were conducted for five years and brought to light a large quantity of objects including the statues known as the "Great Herculense" and the two "Little Herculenses" which the Prince sent to Vienna as a gift for Eugene of Savoy and are now in the Dresden Museum, as well as columns and precious marbles. The government did nothing to limit the excavations until 1716, by which time the precious marble facing from the stage and groups of sculptures had been dispersed among various museums. (Winckelmann records the discovery of the three Herculense statues in a letter to Count Brühl published in Dresden in 1764). It was not until 1738, with the accession of Carlo di Borbone, that excavation work began again. The discoveries that ensued stand as one of the most significant and unifying components of the neoclassic artistic movement, a focal point in the kaleidoscopic history of European culture.

It is hardly surprising that the starting-point for this new campaign of excavations was the theatre. The work, under the direction of first the military engineer Alcubierre, then Bardet (up to 1745), then Weber (from 1750 to 1764) and finally La Vega, was arduous in the extreme for three reasons: the almost impenetrable mass of rock which had overlain the ancient town for 17 centuries, the fact that no one had any idea how much lay buried, and the houses that had been built in the hamlet of Resina directly over the site. In these prohibitive conditions Weber and La Vega made sketches and plans of the buildings they came across in the labyrinth of tunnels burrowed through the rock. There was as yet no orthodoxy for the methods used to bring out the prized works of art: walls were pierced and colonnades demolished without a qualm. As a result, the precious marbles in African, ancient yellow, cipollino and serpentine, and the alabasters, flooring and columns were virtually annihilated. The shafts and tunnels bored to explore the theatre soon led on to one of the ancient town's main public buildings, the Basilica. The years 1750-1765 also saw the start of the excavation of the Villa of the Papyri. Here too explorations proceeded through underground tunnels reached by shafts, under the direction of the Swiss architect Karl Weber, who drew up a plan of the building annotated with his hand-written observations. This gives us a clear idea of both the villa's architectural characteristics and the exact spot where the various finds were made. A remarkable number of artefacts came to light, including about ninety sculptures, numerous frescos, flooring, columns and cornices in precious marble, all now in the Naples Archaeological Museum. The discovery that created the greatest sensation, in November

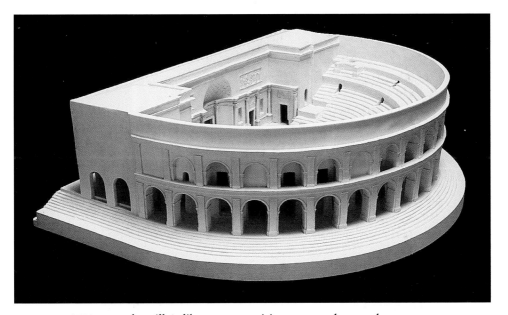

1753, was the villa's library, comprising over a thousand papyrus scrolls containing philosophical works either written or selected by the Epicurean philosopher Philodemus of Gadara. When these finds were published the Villa aroused interest and amazement in Italy and all over Europe for the rest of the 18th and throughout the 19th century, "bringing about a genuine revolution in taste, fashion and furnishing, and giving a great impulse to the movement away from the Age of Enlightenment and into the neoclassical period".

It became obvious that the results of the excavations ought to be publicised throughout Europe and in 1755, on the advice of his senior minister Bernardo Tanucci, Carlo set up the Accademia Ercolanese. The treasures yielded up during the five years of d'Elbœuf's investigations and then during the Bourbon period, from 1738 to 1765, were first collected in the Royal Palace of Portici. At the turn of the 19th century they were moved to

View of the proscenium
of the theatre in Herculaneum

Giacinto Gigante, Visitors
to the Theatre in Herculaneum.
Naples, private collection

Naples, to the building which had formerly housed the
university, Palazzo degli Studi di Napoli, known today as the
Naples Archaeological Museum.

Excavations at Herculaneum were suspended in 1780, following
the discovery on August 16th 1763 (another red letter day for
archaeology) of a marble statue in the locality Civita. This was
the first indication that thereabouts lay the ancient town of
Pompeii. Efforts were concentrated on this new site, where
excavation work was much easier, and the Bourbons had the
satisfaction of seeing Pompeii gradually emerge during the reign
of Ferdinand IV and the Napoleonic interlude (1770 to 1815).

Theatre
(entrance from Corso Resina, 123)

Of the various public buildings known to us in Herculaneum,
the theatre is the only one to which access is still through the
tunnels burrowed by the Bourbon excavators. It lies below
ground: the houses of Resina were built on top of the volcanic
rock formation that overlay the ancient building, and the main
Naples-Castellammare road runs right across this land. The
theatre's arena is 24 metres below today's groundlevel. The
theatre is situated to the north of the site, not far from the start
of the *decumanus maximus*. The terraces face north-west, and
comprise nineteen rows of seats divided vertically into six
sectors. Around the top there is a vaulted corridor, and three
more rows of seats were built above this. At the centre there
was a small temple, of which you can still see the stuccoed
plinths and the drums of its columns. This structure was flanked
by two more plinths, with another pair the same height at either
end of the hemisphere, where there may have been two more
aedicules. This is where the bronze horses stood whose
fragments are now in the Naples Archaeological Museum.
The *proscenium* was decorated with twelve Corinthian columns

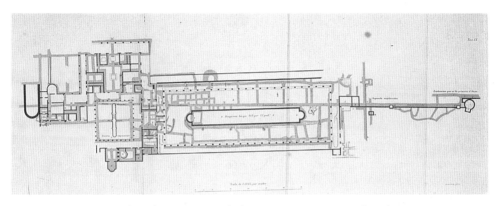

interspersed with recesses and three entrances. At each side plinths bore inscriptions in honour of the consul Appius Claudius Pulcher and the praetor and pro-consul of Crete and Cyrene M. Nonius Balbus.

An inscription from the Augustan era records Lucius Annius Mammianus Rufus as having the theatre built at his own expense, to the design of the architect P. Numisius. The building, restored following the earthquake in 62 A.D., was in stone, with the load-bearing structures in *opus reticulatum* clad in marble panels. The seats were carved blocks of tufa, and the stage was brickwork laid on top of *opus caementicium*.

Villa of the Papyri
(under excavation; adjacent to Via Mare)

On May 2nd 1750 the military engineer Roque Joaquín de Alcubierre informed the senior minister Tanucci that, during the digging of a soakaway near Via Cecere (between Portici and Resina), the workers had come across some ancient remains. This marked the beginning of one of the most exciting episodes of archaeological discovery. The first fruits of the excavation were greeted with rapture by all lovers of antiquity. "It was the major event in humanist culture during that century: the whole world

33

participated in the emotion; and those investigations gave new vigour to the study of antiquity, to research and exploration, which were taken up with fervour, and to the whole cultural and scientific movement that surrounded the art, civilisation and history of the Greeks and Romans".

Starting from the Ciceri shaft, a 400 metre long tunnel was bored, with galleries branching off it. This made it possible, under the vigilant supervision of Karl Weber, to encompass the whole villa, which proved to be very extensive (253 metres by 32).

As the excavation progressed, the Roman maritime villa, familiar to scholars from the description given by Pliny the Younger, left the realms of the imagination and emerged in all its splendour, its rooms decorated in marble and frescos, adorned with a splendid collection of art works, the fine peristyle crowned by thirty six columns, and a profusion of statues and bronze and marble busts. Reality had surpassed the imagination, and thanks to the detailed plan of the building drawn by Weber, scholars were able to describe and expound on it.

Endowed with the spaciousness of an Imperial residence, its main axis comprised the sleeping quarters, a square peristyle, the *tablinum* (reception room), a second, rectangular peristyle and finally a terrace-solarium which opened out onto a circular belvedere raised up and overlooking the garden. It was indeed an ideal residence for a man of culture, with views over the bay and the verdant countryside stretching away behind it.

In 1765 work was suspended on the whole site and the entrance shafts were sealed up. The famous villa, buried beneath a mud and lava flow in 79 A.D. and white hot lava in 1631, remained undisturbed until 1985, when the excavation was reopened to bring it into the light of day. A narrow tunnel was bored beneath Via Mare and part of the spacious premises with halls and a bathing room was excavated, situated just beyond the south-western tip of the town, revealing living quarters, a

courtyard with colonnade and a baths suite with a rectangular
apsidal nymphaeum. Finally the area of the atrium was
excavated, revealing a mosaic floor and a terrace surrounded by
a colonnade and whitewashed, giving onto the bay. Some of the
Bourbon tunnels were cleared, leading to the library and
belvedere. Finds included remains of wall paintings in the II
style, a marble copy of the Borghese Hera and the head of
another statue, a copy of the Amazon attributed to the classical
sculptor Kresilas. Excavation work went on until 1995. At the
moment the site remains closed to the public.

Basilica

The Basilica stands at the intersection of the *decumanus*
maximus and the third *cardo*, on the east side. It is a
rectangular building with a single nave (measuring 16.5 metres

by 29) roofed with wooden trusses. In the far wall, aligned with the entrance, there is a large oblong recess containing three plinths on which stood statues of M. Nonius Balbus and family members. The building can be dated to the Augustan age since the techniques used correspond to those of the adjacent "Temple of the Augustals", whose construction is recorded in inscriptions.

Piazza Porticata (known as the Basilica)

This monument stands on the *decumanus maximus* opposite the College of the Augustals. There have been various conjectures as to its identity, including a forum, temple, basilica, palaestra and curia. Standing halfway along the *decumanus maximus*, its entrance was marked by two large four-sided archways. A rectangular building known as the Basilica, measuring 58.75 metres by 36.5, made a most imposing monument: the inner courtyard had fourteen columns down each of the long sides, and the enclosing walls were supported in the interior by arches resting on semi-columns. The far wall was adorned with three alcoves; in the central square shrine stood a statue of Titus in armour, flanked by two statues, subsequently decapitated, which presumably depicted Vespasian and Augustus. The porticoed area was adorned with a series of statues of the Imperial family and high quality wall paintings featuring mythological subjects. It would have been used both for ceremonies in honour of the Emperor and for major official events, at which most of the township would have gathered.

The site is still below ground, with houses along Via Mare directly overhead. The quality of its decorative schemes and the beauty of the sculpture work put it on a par with the theatre and Villa of the Papyri, the first buildings in Herculaneum to be explored. This excavation began in 1739 under Alcubierre, and was continued by Weber between 1758 and 1761.

Skeletons discovered during
excavations on the waterfront
of Herculaneum

When the Bourbon dynasty was restored, after fifty years of inter-regnum, excavation work began once again in 1828 with Francesco I on the throne. It was undertaken on radically different lines: no longer burrowing down through shafts and tunnels, but opencast, to the east of Vico di Mare, where excavations had already been made. The architect Carlo Bonucci was put in charge of the work, and he directed operations until 1855. His periodical reports, collected by Ruggiero, gave minute descriptions of progress and the new techniques being used. One of the new discoveries was the so-called House of Argos. Once again work was broken off, and began again on the initiative of the young archaeologist Giuseppe Fiorelli, who in 1865 obtained authorization from the Savoy government to carry out further excavations.

In this period two *insulae* and the southern façade of the baths were discovered, a narrow strip of buildings which ran from the southern edge of the ancient town up the third *cardo*. In 1877 digging had to be broken off again and only restoration and maintenance work were carried out. The renewal of excavations in 1927 marked the association of Amedeo Maiuri with Herculaneum. He realised that the populous quarter of Resina was threatening to encroach on land overlying the ancient city, and he made repeated appeals to the authorities to act before it was too late. In 1925 a High Commissioner for the Province of Naples was instituted, and on May 18th 1927 Vittorio Emanuele III struck the first pickaxe blow of the new excavations.

The plan was to begin by exposing the area of the ancient town immediately below the houses of Resina, and then proceed to the modern built-up area above the forum, which being little better than slums was due for redevelopment. The new excavation technique involved digging down transversally from above until reaching the groundlevel of the ancient town. Between 1927 and 1929 the whole area of *insula* III was excavated, including the Houses of the Skeleton, the Hotel, the Wooden Partition and of Craticium. Work then proceeded on *insula* V and its sumptuous residences: the House of the Mosaic Atrium and the House of the Stags, between 1929 and 1932; at the same time the new entrance to the site on Corso Resina was inaugurated.

Between 1931 and 1934 the whole complex of the Central Baths (*insula* VI) was excavated on the landward side of the *decumanus*, and also the lower half of *insula* V with the Samnite House and the Houses of the Furniture, Neptune and Amphitrite and the Corinthian Atrium. From 1933 to 1938 work concentrated on the Palaestra, the House of the Jewel and the House of the Relief of Telephus. Excavation of *insula* V was completed as far as the *decumanus maximus*, and the House of the Bicentenary was also revealed, with its panel bearing a cross. In the years 1939 to 1942

work proceeded on *insula* VI, down as far as the houses of
Resina, and revealed the Houses of the Black Hall and the Two
Atria. Parts of the town walls also came to light, comprising the
earthworks and fortified bastion facing the sea, and a second
bathing establishment, the Suburban Baths, an area with a shrine
and an altar honouring Marcus Nonius Balbus. In this zone
work was held up because of flooding.

After many centuries the town of Herculaneum was being
brought back to life, with its streets laid out on a surprisingly
regular grid pattern, its architectural achievements, its high quality
works of art, and houses belonging to middle and upper class
residents in fine positions overlooking the bay, built using the
latest techniques. Herculaneum has no houses built in the squared

Herculaneum in the 1980s,
from the air

off blocks of stone which are typical of Pompeii. Just occasionally you find such tufa blocks used as the upright in archways, one on the *cardo* opposite the Baths and another in the peristyle facing the House of Argos. The most prevalent building technique is yellow or grey *opus reticulatum*, alternating with layers of tufa ashlar, or more rarely brickwork, *opus vittatum*; in buildings which had suffered lesions in the 62 A.D. earthquake the *opus reticulatum* had been repaired with injections of mortar or tufa ashlar. There are only a few isolated buildings entirely in brick. Excavations were once more interrupted following the Second World War, and did not recommence until 1958. The entire third *cardo* was exposed up to the *decumanus maximus*, but there work had to stop because of the houses of Resina up above, and attention was turned to the palaestra. Beneath those houses lie most of the Basilica, the Civic Basilica, the temples on the Forum and the theatre. This brings us to recent history: in 1975 excavations began again in the area of the Suburban Baths, leading to some extraordinary discoveries. In 1981 the structure of what must have been Herculaneum's harbour emerged from a sand and mud bank, together with the skeltons of a great many citizens who had sought refuge down at the sea and been overcome by the volcanic shockwave. In the following weeks other skeletons came to light, along with other finds, revealing a human tragedy on a scale previously unimaginable. Up until now very few human remains had been found in the town, compared to some five hundred corpses in Pompeii, and it was thought that there had been time for a mass exodus. As excavations went on, however, this hypothesis became ever less tenable. The suburban area revealed evidence of a seaward entrance to the Baths, two gateways into the town from the harbour, two more skeletons and the marble trunk of Marcus Nonius Balbus which had been swept off its plinth. More skeletons emerged in 1982, inside one of the ten chambers built into the retaining wall of the baths terrace. They were the remains of twelve inhabitants who had been trying to escape by sea, which today is some 400 metres away but at that time lapped against the town's fortifications. This made frontpage news, and visitors from all over the world once again took the lively interest in the town's destiny as had been shown in the 18th century. More funds were solicited for extending the excavations, and in the summer of 1982 another sensational discovery was made: a Roman boat which had capsized, with the skeleton of one man, perhaps the rower, nearby and the mortal remains of a soldier not far off. Following the removal of 149 skeletons, work is in progress on displaying casts taken from them using special resins.

The excitement of the discovery led to several initiatives to promote the remains found in Herculaneum. They include the projected underpass leading from the square in front of the modern Antiquarium annexe, where new finds will go on display, to new southern entrance to the site. Visitors will thus approach the town from the sea, as Pliny did.

Itinerary of the visit

Once inside the entrance on Corso Resina, visitors get their first view of Herculaneum from above: a rather unlikely viewpoint, but it does bring home how far the groundlevel in ancient times was below that of today. One is immediately struck by the regularity of the grid plan street layout, with the *decumani* running parallel to the coast and the *cardines* crossing them at right-angles, dividing the terrain up into oblong lots known as *insulae*. The ancient town as we see it extends northwards to the *decumanus maximus*, which marks the boundary between the excavated area and all the rest of the town lying beneath Corso Resina; southwards to the remains of the ancient walls, which from Augustan times onwards were largely incorporated into the villas which the rich had built in this panoramic position;

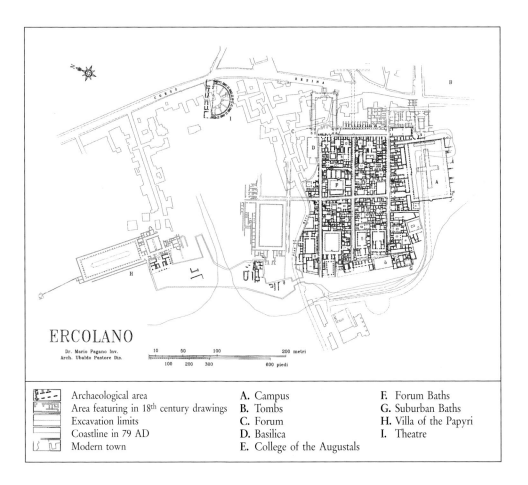

ERCOLANO

Dr. Mario Pagano Inv.
Arch. Ubaldo Pastore Dis.

10   50   100   200 metri

100   200   300   600 piedi

Archaeological area	**A.** Campus	**F.** Forum Baths
Area featuring in 18th century drawings	**B.** Tombs	**G.** Suburban Baths
Excavation limits	**C.** Forum	**H.** Villa of the Papyri
Coastline in 79 AD	**D.** Basilica	**I.** Theatre
Modern town	**E.** College of the Augustals	

House of the Beautiful Courtyard,
small display of finds installed in 1956

westwards to the road leading down to the sea, and eastwards to
the palaestra. Across the middle runs the *decumanus inferior*,
bisecting the excavated area. When you consider that there is
another main street (*decumanus superior*) to the north and two
further *cardines* west of the visible area, all lying under ground,
you realise that the town was in fact much bigger, covering some
twenty hectares, of which we only see five.

Going past the ticket office and down the long shady avenue
which curves round to where the site entrance used to be on Via
Mare, you come to the Antiquarium. This modern building was
planned during the 1970s by the then Superintendent, Alfonso de

Franciscis, as an on-site museum for the objects found here that would give the visitor a sense of where and how the exhibits had been recuperated. The exhibition of finds from Herculaneum (to open shortly) comprises an itinerary of about 850 metres, divided into sections by subject. The first section uses maps, explanatory panels and a photographic display to illustrate the history of the town from its origins to the moment of the eruption. Then there is a small section giving the background of the discovery of the site, featuring photographs, videos and archaeological items, and showing its great impact on the decorative arts in the 18th and 19th centuries. The next section is dedicated to civic life in the

ancient seaside town, featuring above all finds from the
decumanus maximus and the shore. You then go upstairs where
displays of domestic décors and wooden furniture and fittings
give a good idea of everyday life for the townspeople. The final
section has smaller spaces displaying ornaments, the products of
some of the local craftsmen and objects found along the shore,
and a larger exhibition space containing the artefacts coming from
the Villa of the Papyri, including recent finds.
As you leave the Antiquarium, going east, you come to another
modern building, nearing completion, which houses the Roman
boat found in 1982 just off the ancient shoreline. This building

was designed to ensure the security and feasibility of the restoration work, the preservation of the delicate wooden relic and the repristination of the pre-existing reticular Mero node structure. With its two wings in solid brickwork flanking the reticular nucleus, it combines with the Antiquarium to form a single museum complex with complementary spaces. From the panoramic forecourt in front of the Antiquarium you walk across the temporary bridge and find yourself in the House of the Hotel.

Insula II: House of Aristides, House of Argo, House of the Genius
The first building you come to walking up the third *cardo* is the so-called *House of Aristides*. This house, through which the Bourbon excavators brought out the relics found in the adjacent Villa of the Papyri, takes its name from a statue found in the large aristocratic residence, formerly identified as the Athenian politician Aristides but which actually represents Eschine, a famous orator. The atrium and the rooms behind it, up against Via Mare, were built in *opus reticulatum* on the extreme edge of the hill; the rest of the house, which slopes down to the seafront, is built on a massive bulwark in *opus caementicius* clad in *opus reticulatum* and *lateritium*.
Through an aperture made in Bourbon times you enter the neighbouring *House of Argos*, a house of substance excavated between 1828 and 1835 under the direction of Carlo Bonucci. It was named after the fine picture showing Argos guarding over Io, transformed by the enamoured Zeus into a mare, now missing. There is a watercolour by Morghen of the housefront on the III *cardo* showing the magnificence of the interior with its superb peristyle surrounded by a beautiful triclinium and other smaller rooms. On the upper floor, which alas has been almost entirely destroyed, there were a series of small rooms used for storage which opened onto the portico and an internal garden. In these rooms terracotta jars were found containing wheat, lentils, oil and figs.
If you continue along the third *cardo* you come to the rear

entrance of the *House of the Genius*, excavated in the period 1829-1850: it is largely buried beneath the road and takes its name from a statuette of a Genius. Like the *House of Argos*, its main entrance must have been on the II *cardo*. The *insula* terminates, at the junction with the *decumanus inferior*, with a *thermopolium* (eating house) in which you can see the inner room and the serving counter.

Insula III: House of the Hotel, House of the Skeleton, House of the Wooden Partition, House of Craticium, House of the Bronze Herm
The excavation of the *House of the Hotel* was undertaken by

Carlo Bonucci in the period 1852-1875 and completed by Maiuri. This house, built in the Augustan period, south with a panoramic terrace built over vaulted chambers. The main entrance is on the IV *cardo*, with two service entrances on the III.

Just beyond it on the opposite side of the street is the entrance to the *House of the Skeleton*, excavated by Bonucci in 1830-1831. He gave it this name to record the discovery of a human skeleton. Although the house is not very large, it has fine decorative schemes. It was once three separate dwellings, converted at a later date. Turning down the IV *cardo*, you are confronted by the white plasterwork on the well-preserved

façade of the *House of the Wooden Partition*; this house too was formed by converting two former houses into one. The partition that gives the house its name was put up between the atrium and the tablinum, which opens onto the garden, to make a nicely secluded dining room. Next door is the *House of Craticium*, a typical example of a modest dwelling in which the walls have a wooden and cane frame filled in with tufa and lime mortar and plastered over, a technique known as *opus craticium* and described by Vitruvius.

Continuing down the IV *cardo* you come to the *House of the Bronze Herm*, a small house which is strikingly austere, as you

might expect from an Italic house that goes back to Samnite times. The Tuscanic style atrium has at its centre an impluvium made of tufa blocks and coping.

Insula IV: House of the Mosaic Atrium, House of the Alcove, House of the Fullery, House of the Stags

Crossing over the road, you come to the *House of the Mosaic Atrium*, which owes its name to the famous floor in black and white mosaic with geometric designs. It is a well-to-do house in which the succession of rooms, vestibule-atrium-tablinum, is typically Italic. It is very elegant, both for its wall paintings and

House of the Mosaic Atrium,
view of the atrium

architectonic design, and culminates in a fine terrace overlooking
the sea. Going back up the IV *cardo* you see the *House of the
Alcove* which has two entrances, one of them raised above street
level. It was formed from two previous houses, joined by a
hallway that opens onto the vestibule.

Continuing up the IV *cardo*, the *House of the Fullery* is one of
the oldest houses in Herculaneum. At some point it was
transformed so that the owner could conduct his fulling business
on the premises. On the left of the atrium you can see two tanks
for washing clothes. On the V *cardo*, flanked by a stone bench, is
the entrance to the sumptuous *House of the Stags*, named after
the fine marble statues showing stags being hounded by dogs
(the one of better quality was made in Greece). In its design it is
one of the most elaborate houses in Herculaneum: the internal

*House of the Stags, garden
with reproductions of the marble
sculptures, now in the Antiquarium
of Herculaneum*

On the following pages:
Samnite House, view of the atrium

*Interior of a shop next to the House
of Neptune and Amphitrite, on the
IV cardo, with wine jars. On the
floor remains of skeletons*

*House of Neptune and Amphitrite,
triclinium*

*House of Neptune and Amphitrite,
detail of mosaic in the triclinium*

colonnaded garden links the northern sector (vaulted atrium, triclinium and various lesser rooms) with the panoramic quarters to the south, enclosed by a pergola and recreation rooms. The house, excavated by Amedeo Maiuri in 1929-1932, is oriented north-south to make the most of the view over the Bay.

Insula V: Samnite House, House of the Carbonized Furniture, House of Neptune and Amphitrite, House of the Beautiful Courtyard, House of the Bicentenary, House of the Corinthian Atrium, House of the Wooden Shrine, House of the Large Gateway

At the beginning of *insula* V on the IV *cardo* stands one of the oldest houses, the *Samnite House*, dating from the end of the Samnite period. Its fine façade has a doorway surmounted by

Fresco from a shop, ins. VI, 14

*Fresco from the House
of the Carbonised Furniture*

*House of the Beautiful Courtyard,
view of the courtyard*

On the following pages:
*Fountain of Neptune, standing
at the junction of the V cardo
and the lower main street*

*House of the Bicentenary,
view of the atrium*

*House of the Large Gateway,
view of the entrance*

capitals with volutes and palmettes supporting the wooden lintel. The narrow entrance or *fauces* decorated in the I style leads into the splendid Tuscanic style atrium with a loggia, clearly of Greek derivation, running round the top, closed in on three sides with a pluteus between Ionic columns. Next door is the *House of the Carbonized Furniture*, which is unusual in dating from the Claudian period but having an atrium that imitates the loggia enclosed on three sides just mentioned. It is small in size but has high quality decorative schemes in the IV style. Further along is the *House of Neptune and Amphitrite*, named after the beautiful wall mosaic situated in the summer dining room. This building, with the adjacent winemerchants' booth, is one of the best preserved in Herculaneum. The house is decorated with frescos imitating a garden and with a nymphaeum embellished with theatrical masks. Next door to this, still in *insula* V, is another house with an anomalous layout, the *House of the Beautiful*

61

*Forum Baths, changing room
in the women's sector*

*Forum Baths, changing room
in the women's sector, detail
of the mosaic floor showing
Triton amidst sea creatures*

Courtyard. Instead of an atrium this has an internal courtyard
with rooms opening off it, and it does not conform to the
sequence vestibule-atrium-tablinum. As you enter you find
yourself in the service quarters and kitchen decorated in the II
style. From the courtyard, which is on a higher level, a staircase
with a balustrade painted with ornamental motifs leads up to the
first floor. Among the largest and most opulent houses in *insula* V,
facing onto the *decumanus maximus*, is the *House of the
Bicentenary*, named because its excavation was completed in 1938,
two hundred years after the Bourbons began explorations on the
site. The residence of a Roman nobleman, it was divided up into
various apartments, probably in the town's last period, with the
premises situated along the *decumanus* being given over to
commercial activities. On the first floor, in the apartment of the
householders, there was a small alcove where a carbonized
wooden piece of furniture was found, and in the wall a cross
which some scholars take to be an indication of the presence of
early Christians. On the V *cardo* there is the *House of the
Corinthian Atrium*, which conserves the dimensions of building
plots in the town from the Oscan period. The atrium, with three
brick columns down each side, has a floor in *cocciopesto* inset with
flakes of coloured marble. A low pluteum links the columns and
runs round the central impluvium. This is followed by the *House
of the Wooden Shrine*, with a very simple architectonic layout, the
walls in *opus incertum* and the entrance gateway in blocks of tufa.
Its name comes from the cupboard-like lararium found on the
groundfloor together with the bronze seal belonging to L.
Autronius Euthymus. On the *decumanus inferior* there is the
House of the Large Gateway: a fine archway with semicolumns in
brickwork, originally plastered and painted red, surmounted by
Hellenistic capitals in grey tufa showing two winged Victories,
leads into the entrance hall; opposite there is the triclinium with a
high quality painting on the far wall showing a Dionysiac scene.

Forum Baths, passage from changing
room to the warm room
in the women's sector

On the following pages:
Forum Baths changing room
in the men's sector

House of the Black Hall, view
of the garden with portico

College of the Augustals, detail
of frescos in the IV style in the shrine

College of the Augustals, view
of the courtyard and shrine

Insulae VI and VII: House of Galba, Forum Baths, College of the Augustals, House of the Tuscanic Colonnade, House of the Black Hall

The *House of Galba,* named after the bust of this emperor found in the street opposite, stands on *insula* VII, only partially excavated because it has Vico Mare and modern buildings on top of it. The origin of the building is Samnite, as can be seen from the rough hewn blocks used in some of the pillars; a peristyle with tufa columns in the Ionic order encloses a square courtyard, at the centre of which there is a pool in the shape of an X dating back to the Claudian or early Flavian period. The design of this house has no equivalent in any other private building either in Herculaneum or in Pompeii.

The *Forum Baths* (on which excavations began in 1873, being completed in 1931 by Maiuri) are the oldest bathing establishment in the town. Their central position between the two main *decumani* made them conveniently close to the public buildings and forum. The succession of rooms – *apodyterium, frigidarium, tepidarium* and *calidarium* – is the usual one in Roman baths, as is the division into men's and women's sectors. The square building, in *opus reticulatum,* dates from the Julio-Claudian period.

The baths entrance is across a narrow oblong courtyard with walls in *opus reticulatum* lacking any decoration; it is likely that they were being restored when the eruption struck. Adjacent to this courtyard, to the north, is the palaestra, an open-air courtyard surrounded by a portico with brick columns covered with stucco. Beyond is the men's sector of the baths, comprising two vaulted rooms measuring 20 Roman feet across (5.95 metres). The *calidarium* has a hollow floor through which hot air was passed, while the recesses for storing clothes in the other room identify it as the *apodyterium* (changing room). The ceiling is decorated with stucco work and the floor is in white mosaic. Adjacent to the east is a round room, the *frigidarium.*

On the IV *cardo*, opposite the House of the Loom, is the
entrance to the women's sector of the Forum Baths. The vestibule
is adorned with semicolumns and leads into the *apodyterium* with
a barrel vault ceiling and mosaic flooring. A small door leads
through into the *tepidarium* and thence to the *calidarium*.
In the area of the Forum, the heart of the town's political,
religious and commercial life, stands the *College of the
Augustals*, custodians of the cult of the Emperor. This square
building has four Tuscan order columns dividing the central
area into three naves, the lateral ones covered by the carbonized
remains of wooden beams. At the back, facing the main
entrance, there is a shrine with two steps leading up to it,
decorated with frescos in the IV style.
On the *decumanus maximus* there is the rear entrance of the
House of the Tuscanic Colonnade and the main entrance of the
House of the Black Hall, with its orthodox sequence of atrium,
tablinum and peristyle, off which open the large black hall,
whence its name, and two *diaetae*.

Insula Orientalis I

Two houses occupy this area, built on the edge of the
escarpment above the Suburban Baths, to which they are
connected. The *House of the Relief of Telephus* takes its name
from the fine bas relief depicting the myth of Telephus found
inside. In this building the peristyle is on a lower level than the
atrium, on account of the sloping terrain, with a ramp leading
down from one to the other.
The *House of the Jewel*, named after the jewel featuring a
woman's profile from the Claudian period found nearby, is on
the southernmost edge of the town, built on top of an artificial
embankment with chambers built into it. The atrium, with red
and black wall paintings, is in the Tuscanic style and has walls
reinforced with pillars to support the roof. The triclinium opens

onto the loggia overlooking the sea, with two *diaetae* at either
end for rest and recreation.

Insula Orientalis II

The whole *insula* is taken up by the *Palaestra*, with a fine hall
culminating in an apse with the *mensa agonistica*, on which were
displayed offerings to the gods or the prizes for the victors.
There was also a large central pool for the athletes, with water
pouring out of a bronze fountain.
During the Bourbon explorations one of the entrances to this
building, with two columns, was wrongly interpreted by La Vega
as a temple of *Mater Deum*. The building is on the grand scale,
with an elongated rectangular groundplan and two monumental
entrances facing the *decumani*. The street front on the V *cardo*
has a series of workshops and rented accommodation; the
impressive vestibule opens onto the portico, the various rooms

*Suburban Baths, tetrastyle atrium
with central fountain surmounted
by a herm of Apollo*

and the open-air exercise court. At the northern end, adjacent to the *decumanus maximus*, another spacious vestibule leads into an enormous hall and a loggia catering for spectators of the athletic competitions. At the centre of the peristyle a large X-shaped pool has a bronze fountain at its centre shaped like a five-headed serpent twisted round a tree (representing the Hydra of Lerna slain by Hercules). Down in the pool it is possible to see the tunnels bored by the Bourbon excavators.

The *Suburban Area*, which goes from the ramparts down to the sea, is linked with the town by means of two steep alleys descending from the archways at the ends of *cardo* IV and V and joining to form a single ramp that runs down to the waterfront. The *Suburban Baths* were built at a later date than the Forum Baths, to a square groundplan and up against the House of the Jewel and the House of the Relief of Telephus. Excavation of this complex began during the Bourbon period, as can be seen from the gaping breaches in the ceilings and walls. Systematic excavation only began in 1940, conducted by

Amedeo Maiuri, but had to be broken off on account of water infitration, and was restarted in 1952.

The entrance to the Baths is on the western side through an archway with columns and tympanum. The brick columns are surmounted by Corinthian capitals supporting a small pediment with architrave and tympanum, and in the centre you can just make out a mask in the form of a medusa. The square vestibule leading into the baths has a tetrastyle atrium with a column at each corner of the marble impluvium. Above are two orders of semicircular arches serving as a skylight. Between the columns stands a herm of Apollo, in front of which is a fountain with a circular marble basin.

On the beach, immediately below the terraces of part of the Suburban Baths and the so-called Sacred Area, there are a series of vaulted chambers where boats and marine paraphernalia were stored. In 1980-81 excavations brought to light a large number of human skeletons and a horse. These proved to be dramatic evidence of the catastrophe that struck Herculaneum in 79 A.D.: some three hundred townspeople had fled down to the waterfront and taken refuge in these storerooms, only to be suffocated by the pyroclastic shockwave and buried beneath the volcanic debris. The level of the coastline sank following the eruption, so that this waterfront is four metres below the present sea level.

Other finds included gold and silver jewellery and the boat, mentioned above, measuring nine metres in length and three across, in an excellent state of conservation, including the fulcrum of the rudder. Near the boat there were the skeletons of a man, possibly a fisherman, and a soldier wearing his sword and belt, as well as fishing tackle including lines, hooks in wicker cases, and combs and floats for the nets.

Portici

Portici and the Golden Mile

The Vesuvian Villas are splendid creations in which architecture
blends admirably with the environment: in the brief history that
follows, we can trace the ongoing relationship between nature
and architecture, between the villa, the countryside and Vesuvius.
The architecture which distinguishes these villas, rendered
outstanding by the context even when it is quite unassuming,
draws on natural surroundings that have aroused amazement and
admiration in travellers, painters and scholars in every epoch.
The villas, exemplary monuments of late-Baroque splendour built
as summer residences for the Bourbon aristocracy, are situated
between the slopes of Vesuvius and the sea at the start of the old
highroad down to Reggio Calabria. Built in the course of
centuries, they were showcases for the ruling class of the
Kingdom of Naples, and exemplify a continuum of historical,
social, economic and productive elements. Already in the 16th
century the area at the foot of Vesuvius found favour with the
ruling class for the potential it offered for making new and more
profitable investments in agriculture. The centralising policies of
the Neapolitan Viceroy Don Pedro di Toledo had forced the
major feudal landlords in Puglia, Lucania and Calabria to go and
live in the capital city. This in turn brought about an exodus of
the lesser gentry, who created country houses for themselves
beneath Vesuvius, partly for recreation, but also with an eye to
ensuring themselves an income from the soil. The most famous
of these first residences was the Villa known as Leucopetra or
Pietrabianca in Portici, which belonged to the humanist
Bernardino Martirano. He gave hospitality to the Emperor Carlo
V on the latter's return from an expedition to Tunisia.
The most wide-ranging territorial reforms came about during
the 18th century following the construction of the Royal Palace
and Park of Portici, extending south as far as the port of

Granatello and north to the foothills of Vesuvius, with the volcano as its incomparable backdrop. The whole coastal strip began to acquire splendid villas surrounded by ample gardens which, as in the past, looked out over the Bay of Naples. The stretch of the Road to the Calabrias between Resina and Torre del Greco became known as "the Golden Mile". During this century, new elaborate constructions were added to the existing residences, enhancing a natural scenario which never failed to enchant visitors. For this reason we can affirm that the history of the Vesuvian Villas is also the story of this magical enchantment that has conquered travellers in every epoch.

The fashion for spending periods of rest and recreation in the coastal plain at the foot of Vesuvius began in 1738 when Carlo di Borbone, who was to become Carlo III, King of Spain, in 1759, gave orders to build a royal villa in Portici. Over the years this grew in size with the addition of new features and the incorporation of previous buildings so that by the last decades of the century it had taken on its characteristic hemispherical layout with two wings embracing the sea, the Road to the Calabrias passing through its front courtyard. In fact it became a palace rather than just a villa, with a highly original architectonic layout, straddling the public highway so as to benefit from an enormous park stretching down to the sea and up to the volcano behind it. Chronicles of the time relate that this site attracted the sovereign following a chance landing. He and his consort Maria-Amalia of Saxony were crossing the Bay when a storm suddenly blew up and the ship had to seek safety off Portici. Enchanted by the beauty of the place, the King decided he wanted to be able to stay there and gave orders for building work to begin. The area began to be developed, as a result not only of the building of the royal villa but also of the archaeological excavations beginning nearby. The extensive old properties were broken up and exploited: the map

Giovanni Carafa Duke of Noja,
"Topographical map of the City
of Naples and its surroundings",
Naples 1775, sheet 28, detail showing
the Royal Palace of Portici and park

drawn by the Duke of Noja in 1775 gives an idea of how the
villas proliferated. This phenomenon of development has never
ceased, reaching prohibitive proportions in our times.
The typology of the 18th century villas falls into two categories:
– those in which the productive interests were paramount; the
more rustic specimens were up on the slopes of Vesuvius, where
the land was worked, while such properties belonging to the

aristocracy were situated along the Mile itself or its diramations, and featured spacious hallways and a garden or park at the rear; – those in which production was combined with recreation, or which were built solely for recreation; these were down towards the shore, below the Road to the Calabrias, and comprised terraced residences opening onto parks falling away to the sea. The close link between the building and its surroundings, in these pleasure grounds, is underlined by the groundplan featuring a central alley on which the house, garden and estate were aligned. Frequently this succession of elements was laid out with a scenographic effect in mind. The popularity of this area as a summer resort received its first setback in 1860 with the fall of the Bourbon monarchy, and finally died out in the early years of the 20th century.

Another royal initiative associated with the creation of the Royal Palace in Portici was the setting up of one of the most important metalworks in Southern Italy at Pietrarsa, ordered by Francesco II in 1840. There were already precedents for the institution of industrial manufactories on royal estates (as at San Leucio), but the factory of Pietrarsa was part of a more widespread development of metal-working, financed by both public and foreign investments, which transformed the economic outlook of the whole of the coastline from Naples to Salerno. The factory of Pietrarsa was capable of a sizeable output, ensuring its importance even after the Unification of Italy. It was decided to build the new complex on the site traditionally known as Pietra Bianca (Leucopetra), where in Napoleonic times the French had put up a battery to control the sea approach. The toponym changed to Pietrarsa ("burnt stone") following the eruption of Vesuvius in 1631, when the lava flow extended down as far as here.

On October 3rd 1839 the first stretch of railway in Italy was inaugurated between Naples and Portici. The distance, 7406 metres, was covered in eleven minutes by two trains pulled by twin locomotives, the "Bayard" and the "Vesuvio", designed by the French engineer Armand Bayard de la Vingtrie from the prototype by George Stephenson. One hundred and fifty years later, on October 7th 1989, the Railway Museum of Pietrarsa was officially opened. This museum is of outstanding cultural interest both for its environmental and architectonic features and for the historical and scientific importance of its exhibits. It is indeed highly appropriate that the old Bourbon manufactory should be used to display them so close to the original railway line. It can be reached by trains that leave Naples Central Station and follow the old route, drawn by the perfectly restored locomotive "Bayard" in full working order. The original carriages are on display as the first item in the museum in what was once the Assembly shed, complete with its central pit around which are drawn up twentyfive steam locomotives and four electric three-phases, spanning more than a century of railway history. Situated beside the sea, the museum illustrates the history of railways through the length and breadth of Italy. Near the statue of Ferdinando II on the avenue outside there is access to the library, possessing some seven hundred books, and there is also a souvenir shop. The visit terminates in the large shed of the former Turnery, with its pointed gables, full of station memorabilia and reconstructions, some of them large-scale, of stations and rolling stock.

The Royal Palace of Portici
(Portici, Via Università, 50)

In 1738 Carlo di Borbone, crowned King of Naples in 1734, ordered excavations to begin on the site that proved to contain the theatre of Herculaneum, where in 1709-11 quite by chance Prince d'Elbœuf had found the three "magnificent statues" which he gave to his cousin Eugene of Savoy, now in the Dresden Museum. This was the beginning of a new and highly significant era in terms of social impact and scientific and artistic progress, marked not only by the enterprise of the excavations but also by the institution, in 1755, of the Accademia Ercolanese. The King invited sculptors, painters and archaeologists to examine the finds turned up in Herculaneum and Pompeii; leading figures such as Gioffredo, Sanfelice, Vaccaro, Canevari, Fuga and Luigi Vanvitelli, who contributed a lot to the standing of Neapolitan architecture during the 18th century, made sure that the classical artistic heritage then coming to light was represented in the golden age of late Baroque and Rococo architecture in Europe. It was appropriate to create a museum inside the Royal Palace of Portici, in a wing of the former Palazzo Caramanico, where the ever more numerous Roman artefacts from Herculaneum could be kept. Under the direction of Camillo Paderni, the museum was only opened to certain choice visitors, and this provoked the ire of educated travellers such as J. J. Winckelmann, who contributed greatly to the reputation of Herculaneum.

Within the museum various important activities were carried out, in specific departments dealing with the restoration of marble and bronze statues, the unrolling of the papyrus scrolls using a machine invented by Padre Antonio Piaggio, cataloguing and drawing. Visitors who had come to admire the precious finds were also shown the techniques used in restoring and reconstructing some of the rooms that had been excavated, which goes to show just how modern the Age of Enlightenment was in some of its cultural initiatives.

The Royal Palace of Portici was built to the design of Antonio Medrano and Andrea Canevari on a site occupied by two older villas (bearing the names of the Principe di Palena and Principe di Santo Buono). This explains its peculiar layout, straddling the "royal road" which led to the new Road of the Calabrias. The large internal courtyard was bisected by this road, so that

The transfer of the antiquities found in Herculaneum from the Museum of Portici to Palazzo degli Studi in Naples. Engraving from "Voyage pittoresque ou description des Royaumes de Naples et de Sicile" l'Abbé de Saint-Non, Paris 1781-86

there were two ensembles of buildings: the "lower palace", which overlooked the Bay and had a monumental façade, and the "upper palace" which faced Vesuvius. Beneath the arches of the first bridge on the road from Portici there is the magnificent entrance of the "Palace chapel", built with a single nave, an octagonal groundplan and a chancel, originally designed as the court theatre.

The large park, designed and laid out by Francesco Geri with summer-houses, fishponds, *jeux d'eau* and finds from the excavations, was further embellished with more pavilions by Ferdinando IV. With the demise of Bourbon rule, the palace became the property of the Italian state and in 1875 it was purchased by the Province of Naples. Currently the Royal Palace and Park are occupied by the Agricultural Faculty of Naples University, and suffer from being put to a quite different use from the one for which they were created.

The Vesuvian Villas

The Royal Palace of Portici and the villas together make up a

"territorial system". One hundred and twenty villas have been recorded to date, of which the following are among the most representative.

Villa de Bisogno di Casaluce
(Ercolano, corso Resina, 189)

The closest villa to the archaeological site (in the direction of Torre del Greco) is Villa de Bisogno, the property of the Count of Casaluce. The opening up of one of the Bourbon tunnels on the "farm of Bisogno" in 1828 was the first opencast excavation at Herculaneum. The record kept by Tascone states that this farm covered most of the archaeological site, which was expropriated prior to the definitive campaign of excavations, undertaken by Amedeo Maiuri in 1927. The façade of the villa is adorned with stucco mouldings; the entrance hall has a lunette ceiling and is decorated with frescos in typical 18th century taste; all too little remains of the splendid garden.

Villa Aprile, formerly Riario Sforza
(Ercolano, corso Resina, 296)

A little further on, just beyond the built-up area, there is Villa Aprile, built in the second half of the 18th century by Count Girolamo Riario Sforza. He also created a verdant park with statues, fountains and groves containing pretty summer-houses, and this, together with the villa's superb setting, aroused the enthusiastic admiration of many illustrious visitors.
Early in the 19th century the niece of Girolamo Riario Sforza, Giovannina, married to the Austrian general Count Nugent, radically transformed the building both inside and out. What we see now is this later version, with a marble flight of stairs in the French style in place of the Baroque original. Similarly the frescos in the interior were eliminated in favour of a neoclassical decorative scheme which is artistically inferior.

Villa Campolieto
(Ercolano, corso Resina, 283)

Not far from Villa Aprile stands Villa Campolieto. Built between 1755 and 1775 by the Duke of Casacalenda, originally to a design by Mario Gioffredo, succeeded in 1763 by Luigi Vanvitelli, this is one of the few villas to have been completely restored by the Ente Ville Vesuviane, which has its headquarters here.
Gioffredo's design had two blocks intersecting in a spacious covered courtyard, forming four matching suites of rooms. The rear façade opened onto a portico-belvedere overlooking the sea, giving access to the stables and the gardens. In 1763 Luigi Vanvitelli took over from Gioffredo and redesigned the large circular portico as a covered belvedere, making it into an ellipse which harmonised better with the villa. The two were linked by a straight colonnade with a double flight of stairs which led from the first floor to a terrace built over the portico.

The paintings of mythological subjects on the first floor by
Fedele Fischetti and Jacopo Cestaro are particularly fine.
Another of Vanvitelli's innovations was the vestibule
surmounted by an airy dome on the floor above the entrance
hall. He also inserted a ceremonial staircase in marble leading
from the ground to the first floor which recalls the one in the
Royal Palace of Caserta. This villa has been used since 1981 for
cultural and scientific activities of international importance, and
is the headquarters of the business school Iri-Stoà.

Villa Favorita
(Ercolano, corso Resina, 291)

Going on down the street you come to the magnificent façade
of Villa Favorita. Whereas Villa Campolieto is perhaps the finest
of the villas from the architectural point of view, the

neighbouring Villa Favorita has had the most colourful history.
This elegant residence, which bears the magisterial imprint of the
architect Ferdinando Fuga, was built for the Duke of Berrette
and later purchased by the Prince of Jaci, the commander-in-chief
of the Bourbon army. Work was completed in 1768 and the villa
inaugurated to celebrate the arrival in Naples of Maria Carolina
of Austria, the bride of Ferdinando IV. On his death the Prince
left the villa to his sovereign. The Queen renamed it "Favorita"
after the residence she had left behind at Schönbrunn.

Francesco Sicuro, view over the sea
from Villa Favorita, 1777, engraving.
Naples, Museo di San Martino

The architectural design is a triumph of form; its most striking feature is the façade stretching unbroken along the street-front, concealing everything that lies behind it. From the impressive curving staircase that leads down to the panoramic terrace inside you see a breathtaking interplay of colours and volumes, with the grey of the Vesuvian stone, the green of the park and the ultramarine of the sea. In 1823 Leopoldo, one of Ferdinando's sons, supervised the layout of the park and stables and added an additional three-floored building designed by Pietro Bianchi. Following restoration work in 1854, carried out by Enrico Alvino, the villa had Ismail Pasha as an illustrious resident, and the rooms decorated with Arabesque motifs evoke this period of its history. It is currently state property, under the administration of the Ministry of Justice, and the Ente per le Ville Vesuviane is undertaking the restoration of part of the magnificent park which stretches down to the sea and includes a 19th century pavilion and two coffee-houses.

Villa Ruggiero
(Ercolano, via A. Rossi, 40)
This building, shown on the map of the Duke of Noja, was

originally put up by Baron Enrico Petti in the first half of the 18th century, and purchased by the Ruggiero family in 1863. It has rich stucco decorations and is built round a crescent-shaped courtyard decorated in fine Rococo style.

The entrance arch, framed by two bossed pilasters with Ionic capitals, is surmounted by an elaborately wrought balcony. A cross-vault vestibule opens onto the elliptical courtyard. On the first floor there is a harmonious succession of balconies and windows surmounted by gables decorated with scroll motifs. The villa's rear façade has a *serliana* supporting a terrace looking up to Vesuvius and is decorated with marble busts of the Seasons. It has balconies with delicate scroll designs, and is altogether the most interesting feature of the villa. Following restoration work which lasted four years, the villa has been open to the public in all its splendour since 1992.

Palazzo Vallelonga
(Torre del Greco, corso Vittorio Emanuele, 176)

This villa, built in the early years of the 18th century on the site of a 17th century farmstead, had two floors facing onto the street. It was restored in 1843 by Sasso, who added a third floor. At the far side of the courtyard is a massive staircase in volcanic stone (piperno), the only vertical element, which at the first floor branches out to form two flights.

Villa del Cardinale
(Torre del Greco, via del Purgatorio, 122)

This villa was built in 1744 for Gennaro de Laurentis and purchased by Giuseppe Spinelli, archbishop of Naples as a summer residence. It still belongs to the archbishopric of Naples. Its structure is elegant and compact: the street front has two floors, while the internal façade on the courtyard and the park gives onto a sweeping terrace-belvedere commanding a fine view of Vesuvius. The marble staircase, hall, first floor and stucco work are all typical features of an 18th century residence. The large internal courtyard, with an exedra at the far end embellished with recesses and busts, leads through to the garden adorned with stone basins and seats.

Villa Bruno-Prota
(Torre del Greco, via Nazionale, 401)

This villa has an impressive archway surmounted by an aedicule dedicated to San Gennaro. On the façade the discreet outline of the pilasters frames the entrance to the garden avenue and the two side balconies. The main mass of the building is flanked by two wings embracing the spacious courtyard. Unfortunately the overall architectonic harmony was ruined by the building implanted in its midst during the 19th century.

Villa Prota
(Torre del Greco, via Nazionale, 1009)

The original villa was probably remodelled by Antonio Vaccaro, producing an exquisite Rococo building that stands as one of the most striking examples of Neapolitan Baroque.
As you walk down the long avenue through the park, with the villa in front of you, you are constantly taken by surprise with a succession of scenographic close-ups and backdrops. Once through the entrance archway, with its ample vestibule and side balconies, you are confronted by the main building with its fine open stairway and richly embellished façade, surmounted by a flying arch. The large adjacent park is still very beautiful, with lush vegetation running down to the sea.
Going back to the archaeological site of Herculaneum, we now turn in the direction of Portici and Naples, no less rich in important 18th century monuments.

Villa Signorini
(Ercolano, via Roma, 43, from the site of Herculaneum
in the direction of Portici)

The villa, with two floors, has a colourful Rococo façade with
a central archway framed by piperno bosses. The groundfloor
windows are surrounded by stucco scrolls and volutes,
rendered more striking on the first floor. The rear of the
building opens onto the garden with two asymmetrical wings
overlooking a spacious terrace running the whole breadth of
the building.
In the garden full of orange and lemon trees there are two
small arched pavilions faced in 18th century majolica and a
fountain with a statue of Leda. The villa was recently restored
and is the venue for congresses and banquets; inside visitors
can admire the well preserved frescos.

Villa d'Elbœuf
(Portici, piazza San Pasquale, 16)

Ferdinando Sanfelice, whose imprint can be recognised in the elegant elliptical staircase, built this villa in 1709 for Emanuelle-Maurice of Lorraine, Prince d'Elbœuf, who took pleasure in embellishing his splendid residence with archaeological finds from nearby Herculaneum. In 1742 the building and park were purchased by Carlo di Borbone from the Count Giacinto Falletti in order to have a landing-stage for the royal palace nearby. Subsequently Ferdinando IV had the so-called "Queen's Baths" built on the shore below the villa, a small bathing establishment in neoclassical style.

Palazzo Mascabruno
(Portici, via Università, 48-52)

In 1754 work was begun on converting a preexisting building into the Royal Mews, at the orders of Carlo III and to the design of Tommaso Saluzzi. With its four spacious courtyards, this building served as a barracks for troops of the Kingdom and included officers' quarters.

Palazzo Orsini di Gravina
(Portici, via Gravina, 8)

This palace is shown on the map of the Duke of Noja as "Casino e delizie del Vella". It was commissioned in 1754 by Don Vincenzo Lecce together with a chapel dedicated to the Holy Cross and the marvellous park. It subsequently became the property of first Don Vincenzo Vella and then the Duke Orsini di Gravina, who enlarged both the building and the garden, which was the object of an important botanical study by Petagna and Tenore.
It is laid out round a vast courtyard featuring two symmetrical staircases with flying arches. It was a favourite haunt of the Neapolitan nobility, including Queen Caroline of Austria. Particularly fine are the chapel, with the flight of steps leading up to it encased by a stone balustrade, and the gateway in piperno. It was transformed by building work carried out in 1913, and in 1948 it became the headquarters of the Collegio Landriani.

Villa Meola
(Portici, via Marconi, 49)

Built in 1724 for the Count Carlo Danza, according to Roberto Pane by Domenico Antonio Vaccaro, this villa is a fine example of Neapolitan Rococo. The main feature of interest is not so much the streetfront, embellished with an ornate archway, but the courtyard with its richly decorated symmetrical double flight of stairs.

Villa Lauro Lancellotti
(Portici, corso Garibaldi, 227-231)

Designed by the architect Pompeo Schiantarelli and built in 1776, this has a simple, austere façade featuring a rustic bossed sector at the centre which contrasts with the sober decoration of the wings. Inside it has the rich stucco work which was typical of that period, and falls away to the garden down a succession of terraces and steps. The garden has various outbuildings including an exquisite 18th century pavilion with open arches on each of its four sides and fine statuary.

The Vesuvian villas are, as we have seen, an important architectonic phenomenon which, in the course of time, have had an effect not only on the landscape but also on the urban development of the area and indeed on its history *tout court*. The renewed interest in them highlights the need to preserve this heritage which already was threatened by the transformation of the urban infrastructures that took place in the latter part of the 19th century. In that period the Bourbon highway became lined with buildings, giving rise to the irreversible process of conurbation with the city of Naples. At the same time the need arose, and is still acutely felt today, to conserve the most significant architectural features in the area. In the light of these requirements it is appropriate that the restored Vesuvian villas are now the venue for a number of activities and functions. All the initiatives currently promoted in the Villas Campolieto, Ruggiero and Favorita in particular embody a more up-to-date approach to the administration of our "historical patrimony". In this way the individual villas come to form part of the wider patrimony of resources present in the Vesuvian region.
At the moment the Ente Ville Vesuviane and the Local Authority are collaborating on an integrated programme for the revitalisation of the area through an increased tourist flow by exploiting all the region's resources. This project involves the subsystem of the villas as structure-containers for cultural activities; the system will radiate outwards throughout the

territory along itineraries featuring archaeology, the environment, architecture and the arts and crafts. In this context there is a proposal to unify the parks of Villas Favorita and Campolieto, restoring the 18th century gardens which feature on the map of the Duke of Noja. The roads linking the park with the archaeological site will be pedestrianised, and it also hoped to reopen the Bourbon port at Resina. From here a delightful walk through the park of Villa Favorita would take visitors to Villa Campolieto and the site of Herculaneum.

Resina

This toponym has been the subject of much debate: many scholars have linked it to a woman called *Retina* or *Rectina* mentioned by Pliny. Others have maintained that the town grew up around two rustic villas called *Rectina* and *Pollii* (giving the names Resina and Pugliano, a district nearby). Yet there is no archaeological evidence to support either of these hypotheses, and since various philologists and historians deny any connection between ancient Herculaneum and the modern town on the same site, it seems likely that Resina is a medieval toponym and has nothing to do with either Pliny's nobildonna or rustic villas. Around the year 1000 a village which came to be known as Resina grew up on the solidified mud that had buried the Greek and Roman town: although modern Ercolano is built over the remains of ancient Herculaneum, the history of the two towns is actually separated by several centuries. In that period the territory was densely wooded, as can be seen in a painting decorating the altar in the church of Pugliano, in which the only building depicted is a belltower set in a verdant landscape, amidst a group of houses. Above the church the countryside stretched away, dotted with rustic properties and farmland and crisscrossed by rivers and streams. Following the earthquake of 1631 the landscape changed abruptly. A torrent of lava invaded Pugliano and the royal Road to the Calabrias, but miraculously spared the church. In 1699 feudalism was abolished and the boundaries of the Comune were established: to the south, the sea, to the east, the territory of Torre del Greco, to the north, Ottaviano with Somma, and to the west, the territories of San Giorgio a Cremano and Portici. Resina was soon to become famous throughout Europe as news spread of the discovery of Herculaneum, drawing illustrious visitors to the foot of Vesuvius.

In modern Ercolano, which grew up above the ancient site, we should mention the high street, formerly Via Cecere now Via

Roma, which dates from the 18th century. The old Vico Cecere, which took its name from the owner of an 18th century residence shown on the map of the Duke of Noja as the Casino del Cecere, marks the boundary between Portici and Ercolano. The high street played an important role in the history of the excavations, in particular concerning the discovery of the Villa of the Papyri. On May 2nd 1750 one of the workmen in a squad employed by the Spanish military engineer Roque Joaquín de Alcubierre was digging out a soakaway when he came across part of the villa of Lucius Calpurnius Piso Cesoninus. The Spanish officer lowered himself into what became known as the Ciceri Shaft and ordered a tunnel to be bored for 400 metres horizontally. This revealed the full extent of the villa and made it possible to bring out the rich haul of art treasures it contained. In 1765, after access had been improved by burrowing a network of galleries, the site was invaded by a poisonous exhalation of carbon dioxide which put a stop to investigations. Scholars had to content themselves with the diary written up in Spanish by Alcubierre and the plan of the building drawn by the Swiss architect Karl Weber. In June 1980, thanks to indications provided in Weber's plan, the Ciceri Shaft was located beneath the courtyard of Villa Vittozzi and in 1987 excavations started once again.

Corso Resina

Part of the current route of Corso Resina corresponds to the upper main street (*decumanus superior*) of ancient Herculaneum. After the eruption of 79 A.D. the Emperor Hadrian ordered the road to be rebuilt. At the fall of the Roman Empire it lapsed into the state of abandonment and decay that was the fate of all the Roman lands in the west. In 1780, as part of the development projects undertaken by the Bourbons, the road was refurbished and in 1792 the road

*Giacinto Gigante, On the slopes
of Vesuvio, c. 1846, watercolour.
Naples, Museo di Capodimonte*

running through Resina, from Portici to Torre del Greco, was
renamed Corso Ercolano. In November 1875 the "Anonymous
Company of Horse-drawn Railways" obtained a licence to
operate a tramline to Torre del Greco. This service, with two
stops at Resina, began two years later. In 1930, on the stretch
near Villa de Bisogno, the new entrance to the site of
Herculaneum was inaugurated.

Via Mare

This ancient street, which appears in all maps from the 1700s
onwards under the name Vico di Mare, runs through a quarter
which was traditionally inhabited by fishermen. Its history is
bound up with that of the archaeological site, for it lies at the
western edge of the site, facing the III cardo. Even today the
houses of Vico di Mare still overlook and hem in the ancient
town. In order to excavate what is still hidden underground, a

programme of expropriation and collaboration on an international scale is called for, along the lines proposed by the Englishman Charles Waldstein at the beginning of the 20th century; it would then be possible to expose the theatre, the basilica and the temples and buildings on the Forum.

Via Pugliano

From ancient times the rainwater running off the flanks of Vesuvius scoured steep channels which in time became paths and then roads. One of these must have been the *Ribus* of Resina referred to by Capasso, probably corresponding to the current route of Via Pugliano, a street that dates from the beginning of the 18th century which became well known for being the start of the climb up the volcano. What today is Piazza Pugliano was in ancient times a dense pinewood, a classic example of Mediterranean macchia which the eruption in 79 A.D. reduced to a waste of mud and ashes. On this alluvial stratum the original nucleus of the church of Pugliano dedicated to the Virgin was built during the Middle Ages.
On the map of the Duke of Noja the church is represented schematically, but a print featuring in the *Voyage pittoresque, historique et géographique de Rome à Naples et ses environs* (1823-24) by Abbé de Saint-Non gives a fine view of the hillside of Pugliano. In that period the church appeared as a belltower and beside it a portico with four arches, three of which gave entrance to the church, while the fourth had plaques bearing inscriptions set into it. During the second half of the 19th century restoration and restructuring of the square and the church was carried out, and further transformations followed. Following damage caused during the Second World War it was decided to knock down the west front and rebuild it from scratch. The work was completed in 1966 and today's visitor is confronted by a crude approximation of the façade as it once was.

Santa Maria della Consolazione

An important Baroque church built in 1562 by the Viceroy Parafan de Ribera. Inside there is a fine altar with rich marblework and intaglio and a sacristy dating from the 18th century.

Arciconfraternità della Santissima Trinità

The original structure of this building dates from the turn of the 17th century. In 1730 the oratory was completed, its roof with intersecting oval and lobate vaults being a fine specimen not only of the Baroque art associated with Sanfelice but also of the skill of Neapolitan stucco workers. In 1830, at a time of increasing adhesions, a new oratory was started, completed in 1843. In the apse a transept is adorned with two marble columns donated by Ferdinando II.
The remarkable neoclassical crypt was designed by Niccolini, alternating full and empty architectonic elements to good effect.

Santa Maria del Pilar

The chapel of Santa Maria del Pilar stands in one of the most attractive points of the Golden Mile, in contrada Favorita, just off Via Fiorillo. Built in the middle of the 18th century, it has a characteristic façade in piperno stone and the exquisite stucco work which was a trademark of Neapolitan Baroque. Inside it has a single nave and a vaulted roof, and contrast is provided by the polychrome marble adorning the altar.

Torre del Greco

Torre del Greco is three kilometres from Herculaneum, eight from Oplontis and twelve from Pompeii. Its ancient name has not come down to us, and it does not appear on the *Tabula Peutingeriana*, the ancient map on which our knowledge of local topography is based. It seems to have been more or less a suburb of ancient Herculaneum. The coast road running through it linked Neapolis, Herculaneum, Oplontis and Pompeii, where it branched out towards *Stabiae*, *Surrentum* and *Nuceria*.

We do not have much information about this location in ancient times. Signs of human settlement found in a trench tomb near the Torre di Bassano are analogous to the Sarno Valley civilization, placing the origins of Torre del Greco back in the 9th-8th century B.C. It is likely that the Opician people lived in this area from the 8th century B.C., and in the 5th century B.C. the Oschi settled in nearby Herculaneum.

In the era of Roman hegemony this territory was part of the *ager herculanensis*, and thus came under Herculaneum. After the eruption of Vesuvius, this part of the coast was buried beneath a thick layer of ash and abandoned. We know very little about life here up to the Barbarian invasion, apart from the fact that two hamlets grew up, named *Sora* and *Calistrum*. In about the year 1000 the people living along the coast, under constant threat from Saracen raids, gathered together in settlements protected by dry moats or defence towers. There was a string of towers round the coastline of the Bay of Naples, and the one standing between the village of Sora and the contrada of Calastro was known as *Turris Octava*, being the eighth in succession from Naples. As time went on this nucleus expanded and incorporated the fishing village of Calastro. During the Angevin period the village of Torre Ottava continued to grow, and a document from the early 1300s contains the first reference to it as a centre of some importance called Torre del Greco. (Balzano explains the attribute "del Greco" with the

The topography of Herculaneum
and adjacent area in the "Tabula
Peutingeriana", medieval copy
of a late-Roman original depicting
a complete tour of the Empire.
Vienna, Nationalbibliothek

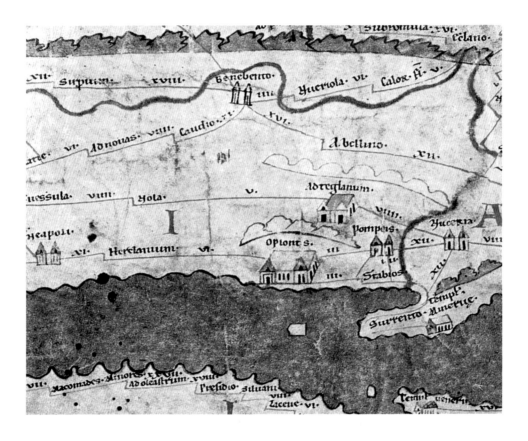

importation of a vine from Greece during the Greek-Byzantine period). Its territory rapidly expanded to the borders with Somma and Ottaviano and the nearby rural hamlets of Resina and Portici. It was owned first by the Carafa family, who were granted it by Queen Jeanne II d'Anjou (1414-1435), and subsequently by the Caracciolo family. In this period this small seaside town fared better than many other towns in the Kingdom of Naples which knew dire poverty; it became important for its coral-fishing activity. When the townspeople liberated themselves from their feudal ties in 1699, it went through a period of prosperity and expansion. At the turn of the 18th century the flourishing coral fishing and coral industry and marine trade in general ensured considerable urban enlargement, while in the surrounding countryside gentry had comfortable villas built. This led to an improvement in the conditions of life in the countryside, and hence progress on the part of the peasants. The population went up to 16,000 inhabitants and continued to grow, thanks not least to the building of the Naples-Castellammare railway in 1841, which gave a boost to the development of the entire region. However, it has to be said that the demographic growth was not conducive to the general well-being of the environment, and it has compromised the status of the naturalistic, historical and archaeological patrimony of the whole coastal region.

The town of Torre del Greco, located at the centre of the Bay of Naples on the southernmost slopes of Vesuvius, was frequently destroyed by volcanic activity. In 79 A.D. this scourge wiped out some splendid maritime villas: one called "Sora" after the locality in which it was situated, and another which is improperly called "Terma-Ginnasio", further damaged during the construction of the railway line (the original Naples-Portici line inaugurated in 1839 by Ferdinando II di Borbone was extended in 1841 as far as Torre del Greco) and by sea erosion. Villa Sora dates from the middle of the 1st century B.C. It was on various levels, falling away to the sea. The first finds came to light in the 17th century, notably the marble bas relief showing Orpheus, Hermes and Euridice in the Naples Archaeological Museum, and a large part of the villa was excavated in the years 1797 and 1798 at the behest of Francesco I di Borbone. This revealed a large absidal room opening onto a portico, with various rooms alongside, a quadriporticus on a lower level and some important sculptures, including the copy of Praxiteles's *Satyr pouring wine* which is in the Palermo Museum. Not far from Villa Sora, some 150 metres to the south-west, can be seen some remains of the so-called Terma-Ginnasio, another terraced building. Here too there is an interesting geo-archaeological stratification which goes back to prehistoric times. In 1989, after a century in which the site had lain fallow, the Soprintendenza Archeologica di Pompei recommenced excavations of the maritime villas in Contrada Sora and Ponte di Rivieccio. This has led to a project for an archaeological park to include the whole district. The project's prime objective is to integrate the areas being excavated with the adjacent land, some of which belongs to the local authority, so as to create a single conservation area. The project for the Archaeological Park of Villa Sora aims to make available to the general public spaces for sport and other leisure activities, didactic initiatives and entertainment, as well as upgrading facilities already in place. Not only will this benefit the urban reality by creating a large archaeological and nature park; the proximity of Herculaneum, Oplontis and Pompeii will make it possible to include Villa Sora in a substantial archaeological itinerary that will certainly attract tourism. The fundamental objective in setting up the park is to rescue qualities which have largely vanished in the rest of the territory of Torre del Greco: gradually all the environmental, natural and architectonic features of the area will be enhanced, including for example the 19th century Villa Montella.

The present reality of Torre del Greco and its territory has little in common with the ancient descriptions we possess. The successive eruptions have radically altered the town's aspect, for it had to be largely rebuilt after eruptions in 1794 and 1861. It covers land rising from the sea to Vesuvius, which can be divided up into three sectors. The first is the low-lying area of the port; the second includes the historical centre and all the important civic buildings such as the Town Hall (Palazzo Comunale) and Coral Museum, as well as the churches of Santa Croce, dating from the early 16th century, and Madonna delle Grazie. The third sector covers the high-lying districts above the trunk road (Circumvallazione). Among various fine monuments we can mention the Castle or Palazzo Municipale in Piazza Plebiscito, about whose origins very little is known for certain. Built at the beginning of the 15th century on a headland rising sheer from the sea, it witnessed the power struggles between the Angevin and Aragonese invaders, and became the property in turn of the noble families of Carafa and Carracciolo. Alfonso d'Aragona had a long stay there, and in fact it was at Torre del Greco that he met and fell in love with Lucrezia d'Alagno. A detailed description dating from 1690 states that the castle was situated at the edge of the Vico di Mare district. It had an open-air loggia or belvedere overlooking the whole sweep of the Bay from Naples to the Sorrento peninsula, round which were grouped various facilities: the stables, men's and women's prison cells, the kitchens and the wash-houses. A double ramp led up to the upper floor with other rooms, the chapel and a loggia with five arches and adjoining panoramic terrace. In 1851 this building became the town hall and was drastically altered: the eastern wing was demolished and the northern wing turned into private apartments. Below the castle lies the quarter of Vico di Mare with its narrow alleyways and

external staircases buttressed by flying arches, typical features of
coastal villages in this part of the Mediterranean.

Another significant monument is the Torre di Bassano, situated
in contrada Sora in Via De Gasperi alla Litoranea. The tower
was part of a system of defences erected by the Viceroy de
Ribera with watchtowers ringing the Bay. Situated in a
commanding position on a rocky headland, it is foursquare with
thick walls and external scarps. Inside on the groundfloor there
were storerooms, on the first floor billets for the guards and on
the second a terrace with gun emplacements.

During the 17th and 18th centuries the town was prosperous

*Parure in Mediterranean coral
and gold, made at Torre del Greco
in the 19ᵗʰ century.
In the necklace the features
of Dionysus, Ceres and Flora can be
identified, with a head of Bacchus,
a mask of Pan and a recumbent
faun. Torre del Greco,
Liverino collection*

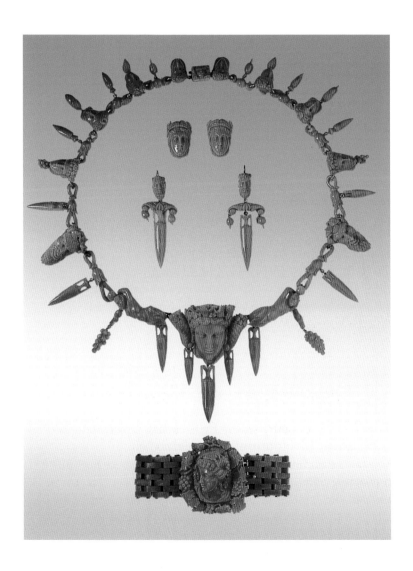

enough to build and furnish several churches adorned with fine fittings and works by famous Neapolitan artists.

Coral

In his *Naturalis Historia* Pliny devotes considerable space to coral, describing its ornamental and therapeutic uses amongst other peoples and giving a detailed description of the places in which it could be gathered, mentioning Campania and a site off Naples. For the local inhabitants, diving for coral and sponges was a staple means of sustenance in view of the fact that the countryside, constantly threatened by the volcano and often destroyed and parched up, produced very little. Although this diving was a long-established tradition, Torre del Greco was not the only centre in this part of the Mediterranean. Since medieval times this activity was also carried on in Genoa, Trapani and Provence, although production there was severely curtailed following the French Revolution. There was also a well-rooted tradition for working coral in Naples, for it was actively encouraged during the Aragon rule in the 15th century.
Boats would set out from Torre for Sardinia, Sicily and the coast of North Africa, shipping the raw material to the various cities where it was worked: Barcellona, Genoa, Marseilles and Trapani. The risks they faced from marauding Saracens and the unfavourable prices for the raw material gradually induced the inhabitants of Torre to set up on their own. Trade was so flourishing that in 1794 the Bourbon government issued a series of laws which were collected in a code known as the "Codice corallino". There was also an attempt to set up a Royal Coral Company but it failed, perhaps because the norms regulating the exchange between gathering and working were too rigid and restrictive for contemporary practice. The first factory for coral working opened in 1805, on concession from Ferdinando IV di Borbone. The French businessman Paolo Bartolomeo Martin,

from Marseilles, secured the exclusive right to work coral for ten years, and this pioneering enterprise showed the way for a flourishing trade which is still in existence.

In 1878 the Naples Chamber of Commerce and the Comune of Torre del Greco jointly set up the "Royal School of Coral Engraving" in the ex-monastery of the Carmelites. Pupils were taught the skills of working not only coral but also lava stone, shells, ivory and semiprecious stones. Visitors can admire the products of this prestigious tradition in the Museo Liverino, which exhibits a range of modern coral artefacts, both local and from China and Japan, alongside historical pieces dating as far back as the 16th century. In recent years production has concentrated on jewellery, involving semiprecious stones and mounted coral. Moreover, coral is not restricted to ornaments, for it is also used in pharmacy. When mixed with other substances it can help to cure various ailments including migraines and digestive troubles and also promotes scar-forming.

Projects for the development of the Vesuvian area, upgrading the archaeological site of Herculaneum

Among the various museums and urban sites which attract tourists to the Vesuvian area, the archaeological park of Herculaneum has long been the most popular venue. Approximately one third of the ancient town has been excavated, and it offers a rich cross-section of private houses and public buildings covering some six hectares of ground. Currently excavators are concentrating on the western zone, towards Portici, along what was the sea front in ancient times, going out as far as the Villa of the Papyri. To the north excavations are made impossible by the urban development that has spread over the buried town in modern times. To the east excavations could be undertaken with the certainty of finding new remains.

In the immediate future the archaeological park of Herculaneum will be provided with new itineraries for visitors, a new entrance and facilities in order to enhance it as a tourist attraction. The programme for upgrading infrastructures throughout the Vesuvian area, with special attention to the Comune of Ercolano, includes new highways linking the motorway with the coast road and the archaeological site in order to speed up traffic, which at present is unduly congested. It also envisages car parks and a landing stage so that tourists can arrive by sea.

In order to limit the problems of urban congestion, the local council is currently completing work which will give improved access to the archaeological site. An area providing ample parking for cars and coaches will communicate with a walkway inside the site leading to a new entrance with a ticket office, educational department and information point all sited round an internal courtyard.

In view of this it has been necessary to identify and plan for spaces, within the site itself, where further visitor facilities can be installed. In the entrance foyer of the Antiquarium, due to open shortly, there will be a bookshop with guides, catalogues, posters and postcards on sale concerning the Vesuvian archaeological sites and Herculaneum in particular. Another space is being created near the panoramic terrace in the outbuildings of the former entrance on Via Mare. It will contain a cafeteria where visitors can relax in an impressive vantage point overlooking the ancient town. Another project concerns the archaeological, environmental and urban upgrading of the hillside to the north of the site by redesigning the layout of Corso Resina and creating new itineraries both above and below ground: the latter will provide access to the ancient theatre directly from the site. To the south it is intended to install a new access bridge linking the panoramic terrace to the III cardine in order to enhance the whole hillside overlooking the ancient sea front. The overall effects of these projects should set in motion a genuine enhancement of the archaeological park of Herculaneum in its entirety.